INSIDE YOUR AMAZING SPIDER-MAN ANNUAL...

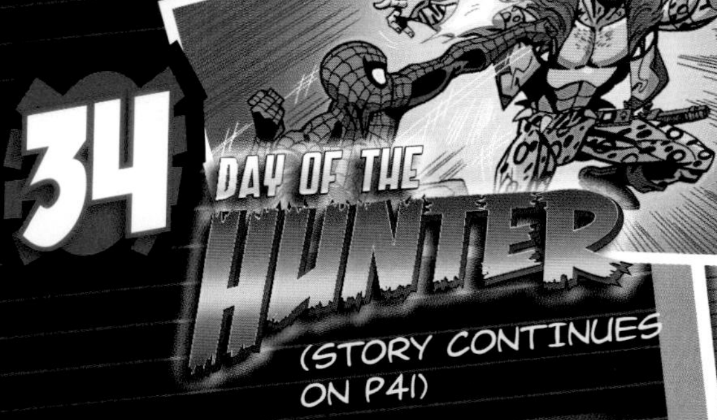

£7.99

BOWLING WITH MARY JANE AND THE GANG, FOLLOWED BY PIZZA AND SHAKES AT LUCIANO'S. YEP, NIGHTS OUT DON'T GET MUCH BETTER THAN THAT.
SO, I'M FEELING PRETTY CHIPPER. UNTIL...
...UNTIL I'M ABOUT TEN YARDS FROM HOME, AND THE SPIDER-SENSE SUDDENLY KICKS IN!
SOMEONE'S THERE ALRIGHT. AND WHEN HE STEPS OUT OF THE SHADOWS, MY HEART STARTS RACING...
...'COS HE MIGHT NOT BE POWERED UP, BUT THAT'S FLINT MARKO - - BETTER KNOWN AS THE SANDMAN!
WANNA WORD WITH YA, PARKER. RIGHT HERE AND NOW.
OMIGOD! SECRET IDENTITY'S BLOWN, LIFE'S IN RUINS...
SANDMAN STRIKES!
SCRIPT: FERG HANDLEY
PENCILS: CARLOS GOMEZ
INKS: GARY ERSKINE
COLOURS: JAMES OFFREDI
LETTERS: WILL LUCAS
EDITOR: PAT BISHOP

...UNLESS I CAN SOMEHOW BLUFF MY WAY OUT OF THIS!
ER, I THINK YOU'VE GOT THE WRONG GUY HERE, MISTER.
NAH. YER PETER PARKER, YA WORK FER THE DAILY BUGLE AN' YER ALWAYS SNAPPIN' SPIDER-MAN IN ACTION.
PHEW, IDENTITY'S SAFE THEN. BUT I'M STILL GETTING ONE NASTY FEELING HERE.
NOW, YA KNOWS I'M THE SANDMAN. WELL, I'VE JUST BUSTED OUTTA JAIL, SO I NEED CASH TA...
SO WHAT IS THIS? A MUGGING?
NOPE, JUST BUSINESS. SEE, SOME A' YER WALLCRAWLER PIX HAD ME IN 'EM, AND I WANT MY CUT... FER THE IMAGE RIGHTS.
BUT THEY WERE PUBLIC DOMAIN. AND BESIDES, I BARELY GOT MINIMUM RATES FOR THEM.
WHAT WITH JOLLY JONAH BEING SUCH A TIGHTWAD...
DON'T LIE TA ME, KID. MIDNIGHT FRIDAY, YER GONNA MEET ME AT BATTERY PARK... WITH TEN GRAND IN HARD CASH.
BY THE WAY, I BEEN CHECKIN' YA OUT. SO MESS WITH ME AN' I'LL GET YA... PLUS YER FRIENDS AN' FAMILY.

THE NEXT FEW DAYS ARE THE PITS. NORMALLY, A BIT OF WEBSLINGING STRAIGHTENS ME OUT...
...BUT WHEN I GO OUT ON PATROL, ALL I CAN THINK OF IS MARKO'S THREATS...
...AND THEY'VE GOT ME WORRIED SICK.
NOT FOR MYSELF, NATCH. BUT THE THOUGHT OF THAT MONSTER HARMING AUNT MAY OR MARY JANE...
...WELL, IT'S A NIGHTMARE. A LIVING, STINKING, GUT-WRENCHING NIGHTMARE.

COURSE, I TRY AND ACT NORMAL WHEN I'M WITH THE GANG. BUT...
PETER, YOU OKAY? YOU'VE BARELY SAID A WORD ALL NIGHT?
MJ'S RIGHT, BUDDY. SO WHAT GIVES?

LOOK, I'M FINE. HONEST, HARRY, I'VE JUST GOT A BUNCH OF COLLEGE STUFF ON MY MIND.
AW, ALL THEM GEEKY FORMULAS GETTING YOU DOWN, PARKER?

CUT IT OUT, FLASH. SERIOUSLY, YOU'RE ABOUT AS FUNNY AS THE HULK WITH TOOTHACHE.
SEE, NORMALLY ITS ME MAKING WITH THE ONE-LINERS. BUT NOT NOW, NOT WITH SO MUCH AT STAKE.

ANYHOW, I DECIDE TO MAKE THE MEET. STILL NOT SURE HOW TO PLAY IT, BUT IT'S DEFINITELY A COSTUME JOB.
KLIK

THE RAIN'S BEEN HAMMERING DOWN ALL DAY. STILL NO LET UP AS I REACH THE PARK, BUT THERE HE IS...
HEY, MARKO. PARKER COULDN'T MAKE IT, SO YOU'RE JUST GONNA HAVE TO DEAL WITH YOURS TRULY INSTEAD.

HAD A FEELIN' HE'D GO BLABBING' TA YA, WALLCRAWLER. THAT'S WHY I GRABBED ME A BARGAININ' CHIP.

AIN'T THAT RIGHT, THOMPSON!
OH BOY, THAT'S THROWN A SPANNER IN THE WORKS. AND IT'S ALL MY FAULT...

...MOPING AROUND WHEN I SHOULD'VE BEEN LOOKING OUT FOR MY FRIENDS.
SO HERE'S THE DEAL. YER GONNA GET ME THAT TEN GRAND, EVEN IF YA HAVE TA ROB IT...
...AN' IF YA DON'T, I'M GONNA PUT THE HURT ON LAUGHIN' BOY HERE.

EITHER THAT, OR YA UNMASK FER ME. SAME DIFFERENCE, 'CEPT I MAKE THE DOUGH FROM SELLIN' THE PHOTOS.
JUST SWELL. MARKO'S GOT ME OVER A BARREL HERE...
...AND IF I MAKE A MOVE, FLASH'LL BE ON A ONE-WAY TICKET TO THE EMERGENCY ROOM!
UH-OH, I RECOGNISE THAT LOOK...
MAN, YOU'RE DUMB. SERIOUSLY, SPIDEY'S GONNA WIPE THE FLOOR WITH YOU!
SIMMER DOWN, PUNK, OR I'LL...
NO WAY! GET OFFA ME, YOU BIG APE!
HUH?
BAD MOVE, THOMSON. 'COS NOBODY MESSES WITH THE SANDMAN!
OKAY, THERE'S MY OPENING. BUT I NEED TO MOVE FAST...

CONTINUED ON PAGE 13

10 THINGS YOU DIDN'T KNOW ABOUT SANDMAN

1.

He calls himself **Flint Marko,** but his real name is actually **William Baker.**

2.

He can mould his sandy body into any **continuous** shape he can think of!

3.

The first time **Spidey** fought **Sandman,** he defeated him by sucking him into an industrial vacuum cleaner!

4.

His first comic appearance was in **Amazing Spider-Man #4** way back in 1963.

5.
He can absorb other grains of sand around him into his own body, increasing his size and volume.
6.
He could've been a pro **American football player,** but ruined his chances by accepting money to lose an important game.
7.
He is vulnerable to high temperatures, which can turn the sand in his body into **glass!**
8.
Once he teamed up with Hydro-Man, only to accidentally combine with him, forming a monster called Mud-Thing!
9.
He can lift up to **85 tons** when he's in his sandy form.
10.
Even if his body is scattered, he still has mental control of all grains of sand that belong to him, allowing him to reform.

SPIDEY CENTRAL!

Help out Spidey by solving these puzzles!

SHAPE SHIFTING!

A

B

C

SANDMAN CAN FORM ANY SHAPED WEAPON HE CAN THINK OF WITH HIS FISTS!

CAN YOU MATCH THE WEAPONS TO THE HOLES THEY'VE MADE IN THE WALL?

NAME & SHAME!

SPIDEY'S HAVING TROUBLE REMEMBERING SANDMAN'S OTHER NAME!

HELP HIM BY CROSSING OUT ALL THE 'SANDMAN' WORDS IN THE GRID, THEN WRITE THE LETTERS YOU'RE LEFT WITH IN THE SQUARES BELOW TO REVEAL HIS ALIAS!

S A N D M A N F S A N D M A N
L S A N D M A N S A N D M A N
S A N D M A N S A N D M A N I
N S A N D M A N S A N D M A N
S A N D M A N T S A N D M A N
S A N D M A N M S A N D M A N
S A N D M A N S A N D M A N A
S A N D M A N S A N D M A N
R S A N D M A N S A N D M A N
S A N D M A N K S A N D M A N
S A N D M A N S A N D M A N O
S A N D M A N S A N D M A N

ANSWER

CONTINUED FROM PAGE 9

...BUT WE ONLY MAKE ABOUT A HUNDRED YARDS BEFORE...
S-SPIDEY?
YEAH, I KNOW. COME ON, THIS WAY.
BIG MISTAKE, MOOKS. 'COS NOW YER DOWN HERE, YA AIN'T EVER GETTIN' OUT AGAIN!
WE MAKE A FEW MORE TURNS, BUT SUDDENLY THERE'S A SOUND LIKE WET GRAVEL AND...
HA HA! GOT YA NOW, BUG-BOY!
FLASH, RUN - - I'LL TRY AND HOLD HIM OFF!
SMASH
NAH, DON'T THINK SO!
IMPACT'S LOOSENED UP THAT BRICKWORK. GOT TO GET THIS JUST RIGHT THOUGH...
FWIPP
NAA ARGH!
KRASH

WAY TO GO, SPIDEY, THAT'S SHOWN THE CREEP.
DUDE, WE'LL BE LUCKY IF IT BUYS US TEN SECONDS.

BUT, I THINK I KNOW HOW TO REALLY STOP HIM.
COOL. SO WHAT DO YOU WANT ME TO DO?
FWIPP
FWIPP
FWIPP

NOT A LOT. JUST GET UP THERE AND HOLD ON TIGHT.

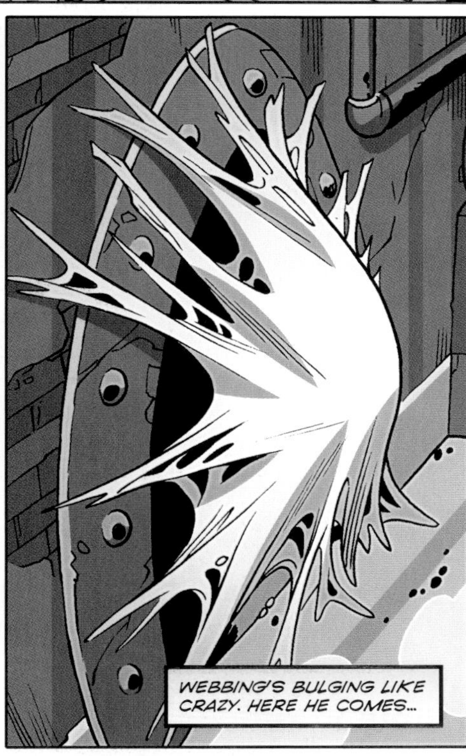
WEBBING'S BULGING LIKE CRAZY. HERE HE COMES...

KRRRK
YER DEAD MEAT, WALLCRAWLER. YA HEAR ME?!
SURE. EXCEPT, THIS IS A MAIN OVERFLOW VALVE. AND YOU MIGHT'VE NOTICED ALL THE RAIN UP TOP.
CREAK

YEP, TOTALLY SLURRIFIED.
WHOA!!
YAAAAARGH!
FWOOSH
OKAY, FLASH, I NEED YOU TO GET TOPSIDE AND CALL THE COPS. TELL THEM TO HEAD TO THE MAIN DETENTION BASIN, OVER BY SOUTH STREET.
SURE, SPIDEY, NO PROBLEMO.

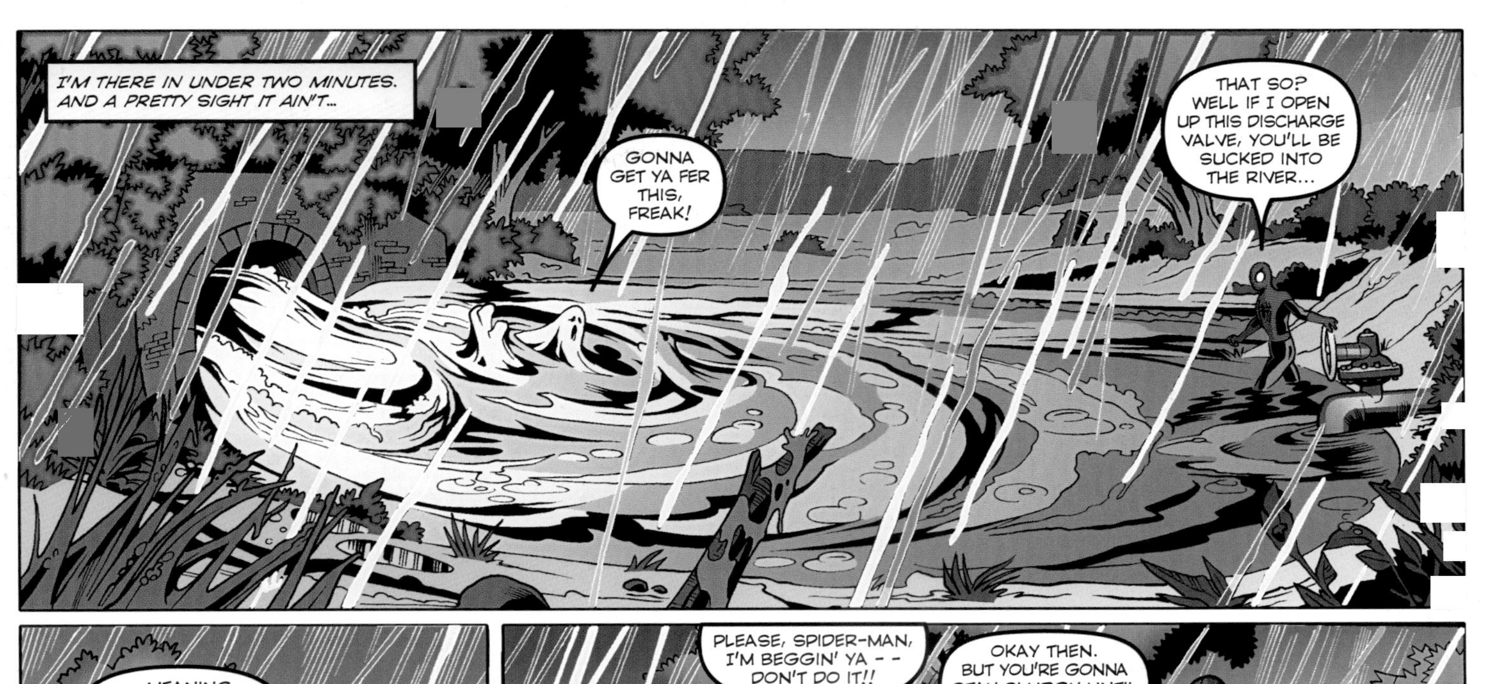
I'M THERE IN UNDER TWO MINUTES. AND A PRETTY SIGHT IT AIN'T...
GONNA GET YA FER THIS, FREAK!
THAT SO? WELL IF I OPEN UP THIS DISCHARGE VALVE, YOU'LL BE SUCKED INTO THE RIVER...

...MEANING IT'LL BE MONTHS, MAYBE YEARS, BEFORE YOU PULL YOURSELF BACK TOGETHER AGAIN.
NO, WAIT!

PLEASE, SPIDER-MAN, I'M BEGGIN' YA - - DON'T DO IT!!
OKAY THEN. BUT YOU'RE GONNA STAY SLUDGY UNTIL THE COPS GET HERE, UNDERSTOOD?

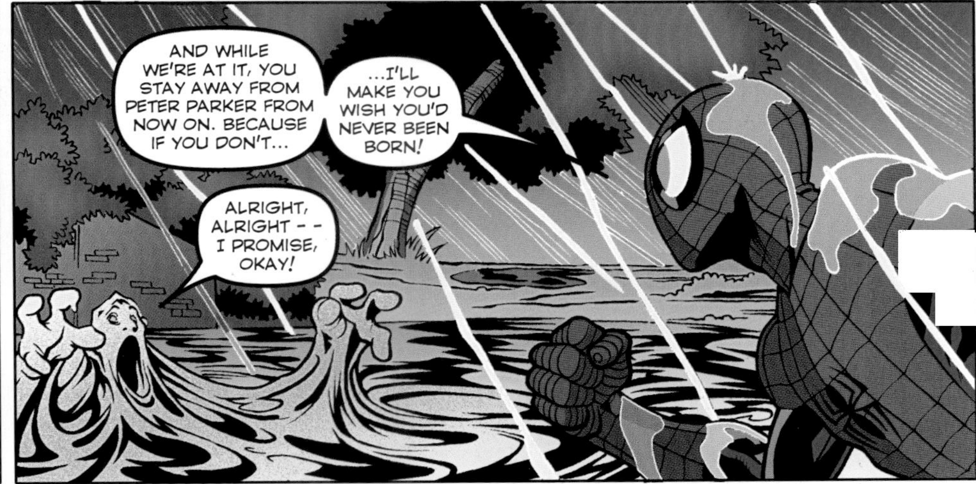
AND WHILE WE'RE AT IT, YOU STAY AWAY FROM PETER PARKER FROM NOW ON. BECAUSE IF YOU DON'T...
...I'LL MAKE YOU WISH YOU'D NEVER BEEN BORN!
ALRIGHT, ALRIGHT - - I PROMISE, OKAY!

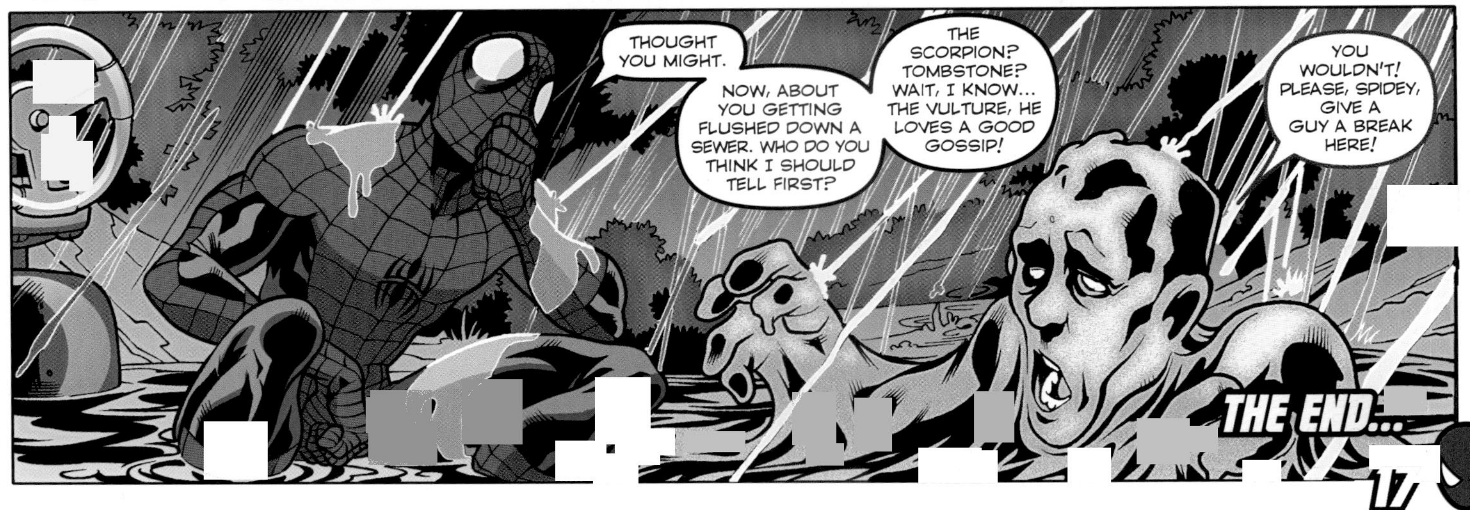
THOUGHT YOU MIGHT.
NOW, ABOUT YOU GETTING FLUSHED DOWN A SEWER. WHO DO YOU THINK I SHOULD TELL FIRST?
THE SCORPION? TOMBSTONE? WAIT, I KNOW... THE VULTURE, HE LOVES A GOOD GOSSIP!
YOU WOULDN'T! PLEASE, SPIDEY, GIVE A GUY A BREAK HERE!
THE END...

SPIDER FILE:
ONE MOMENT HE'S A LIKEABLE SCIENTIST, THE NEXT HE'S A SPIDEY-CRUSHING REPTILIAN MONSTER - TALK ABOUT TWO FACED! IT'S THE...
LIZARD
BLOWN APART!
When Dr. Curt Connors lost his right arm, he tried to grow it back by studying the secrets of reptile regeneration.
CURED?
Eventually he managed to create a serum that grew back his arm, but there was just one tiny little side effect...
A MONSTER!
...Whenever Connors became stressed, he mutated into a giant, bloodthirsty lizard! Okay, so that's quite a big side effect really.
Can control the minds of all reptiles within a mile!
Can grow back his limbs if they're cut off!
Can lift up to 12 tons!
Can whip his tail at speeds of up to 70mph!
Can scale vertical walls just like Spidey!
Scaly skin makes him more resistant to injury than Spidey!
Vulnerable to very cold temperatures due to his cold blood.

I'VE BEEN ON A FEW FIELD TRIPS IN MY TIME, BUT NOTHING LIKE THIS ONE. BECAUSE IN A FEW MINUTES TIME, WE'LL BE TOUCHING DOWN...
...IN THE SAVAGE LAND!
YEP, IT'S HARD TO BELIEVE A PLACE LIKE THIS ACTUALLY EXISTS, ESPECIALLY IN ANTARCTICA. BUT IT'S SURROUNDED BY VOLCANOES, WHICH KEEP THE CLIMATE TROPICAL...
...AND BECAUSE IT'S SO ISOLATED, THE WILDLIFE HASN'T EVOLVED BEYOND THE PREHISTORIC STAGE. SO WE'RE TALKING WOOLLY MAMMOTHS, STONE AGE TRIBES...
RUMBLE IN THE JUNGLE
...AND BEST OF ALL -- DINOSAURS!!!
ENCILS: CARLOS E. GOMEZ INKS: GARY ERSKINE COLOURS: JAMES OFFREDI SCRIPT: FERG HANDLEY LETTERS: WILL LUCAS EDITOR: PAT BISHOP

TARTED AT EMPIRE STATE UNIVERSITY. CURT CONNORS WAS LOOKING FOR A ARY RESEARCH ASSISTANT, SO...
WELL, PETER, I'VE KNOWN YOU FOR A WHILE NOW. AND YOU'RE THE BEST CANDIDATE, SO THE JOB'S YOURS.
THANKS DOC, THIS IS AWESOME!
THE WORK WAS FASCINATING...
...AND I WAS EVEN GETTING PAID, WHICH WAS HANDY.
BUT THEN...
THIS IS FANTASTIC. THE AMERICAN SCIENCE ACADEMY IS PLANNING A RESEARCH TRIP TO THE SAVAGE LAND, AND I'VE MANAGED TO GET ON BOARD.
AMERICAN SCIENCE ACADEMY
THAT SET THE ALARM BELLS RINGING. BECAUSE CONNORS HAS SPENT YEARS TRYING TO REGENERATE HIS MISSING ARM WITH REPTILE DNA...
...BUT ONE OF HIS EXPERIMENTS BACKFIRED, TRANSFORMING HIM INTO THE LIZARD...
...WHO PERIODICALLY RE-EMERGES TO CAUSE MAYHEM AND MISERY.
THEN I CHECKED HIS FILES...
...AND SURE ENOUGH, HE WANTS TO USE THE TRIP TO OBTAIN DINOSAUR DNA, HOPING IT WILL BE PURER THAN THE MODERN-DAY, REPTILE VARIETY.
THING IS, THE DOC'S A DECENT GUY. SO I PERSUADED HIM TO TAKE ME ALONG...
...MEANING I CAN KEEP MY EYE ON HIM IN THIS CRAZY PLACE.

THREE DAYS ON AND THE CAMP'S LOOKING GOOD. THERE'S EVEN AN ELECTRICAL ENERGY FENCE TO WARD OFF NIGHT INTRUDERS...
...AND THIS BEING AN AREA OF UNIQUE BIO-DIVERSITY, THE SCIENTISTS HAVE ALREADY FOUND SEVERAL 'NEW' SPECIES OF PLANTS AND INSECTS.
AND AS FOR THE DOC? WELL, NATURALLY, HE'S FASCINATED BY ALL THE DINOS...
PETER, QUICK - YOUR CAMERA!
ON IT.
...BUT HE'S ALSO ACTING PRETTY STRESSED. AND THAT'S IN PUBLIC...
TOO LATE. DARN IT, PETER, I'VE SEEN SLOTHS WITH BETTER REACTIONS!
...SO I HATE TO THINK WHAT HE'S LIKE ON HIS OWN...
SSSTOP FIGHTING ME, CONNORSSS. THE CREATURESSS OF THIS LAND ARE MY BRETHREN, AND I WISSSH TO JOIN THEM!
NO, GO AWAY! CAN'T YOU JUST LEAVE ME IN PEACE?!
NEVER! FOR MY DAY ISSS COMING, CONNORSSS...
...COMING SSSOON!!!

DAY FOUR, AND WHEN I SURFACE FOR BREAKFAST...
SAY, JERRY, HAVE YOU SEEN DOC CONNORS ANYWHERE?
DON'T ASK ME, BUDDY, I'M JUST THE PILOT.

ACTUALLY, PETER, HE'S HEADED OUT. BUT HE WON'T HAVE GONE FAR, NOT ON HIS OWN.
I SEE. THANKS, PROFESSOR ROSENBAUM.

CONNORS' LOG, APRIL FOURTEENTH. ATTEMPTS TO OBTAIN DNA FROM RESIDUAL SAMPLES HAVE PROVED INEFFECTIVE...

...SO I AM NOW CONCENTRATING ON LIVE HOSTS. THE LARGER SPECIES ARE FAR TOO DANGEROUS OF COURSE, BUT IF I CAN--

WAIT, THIS IS PERFECT. 'RAPTOR EGGS...

...SO ALL I HAVE TO DO IS EXTRACT SOME CELLS AND- -

CONTINUED ON PAGE 26

SPIDEY

SECURITY BREACH!

THE SCIENTISTS NEED TO TURN ON THEIR CAMP'S SECURITY SYSTEM, BUT THEY CAN'T REMEMBER THE 5 DIGIT CODE!

WORK OUT THE ORDER THAT THE NUMBERS WERE PRESSED LAST TIME TO REVEAL THE CODE!

HINT: THE BUTTON WITH THE WARMEST FINGERPRINT WAS PRESSED LAST, AND THE COLDEST, FIRST!

TEMPERATURE 0 100

CODE

DOYOUTHINK-HESAURUS?

TOO LATE! SOME DINOSAURS HAVE GOT PAST THE SECURITY FENCES!

HOW MANY DINOSAURS CAN YOU SPOT THROUGH THE VISION EQUIPMENT BELOW?

NUMBER OF DINOSAURS

CENTRAL!

Help Spidey avoid a dino-disaster by solving these puzzles!

DINO DASH!

CAN YOU FIND A ROUTE FROM START TO FINISH THAT AVOIDS ALL OF THE DINOSAURS?

CONTINUED FROM PAGE 23

MOVE, PEOPLE! HEAD FOR THE CAVE AT THE EDGE OF THAT BLUFF!
SPIDER-MAN! BUT HOW...?
SHORT VERSION? SECRET MISSION, HAPPENED TO BE PASSING BY.
NOW RUN, ALREADY!!!
SAY, THOSE GUYS MOVE PRETTY FAST FOR SCIENCE GEEKS. AND LUCKILY, I PACKED A DOSE OF CONNORS' ANTI-SERUM, WHICH WILL TURN HIM BACK TO NORMAL...
...PROVIDED IN CAN GET IN CLOSE ENOUGH TO FORCE IT DOWN HIS SCALY NECK.
SSSPIDER-MAN!!!
AW, LIZZY -- YOU FORGOT TO SAY 'SSSPECTACULAR' AGAIN. I'D EVEN HAVE SETTLED FOR 'SSSENSATIONAL', SEEING AS IT'S YOU.
PAH, I HAVEN'T TIME FOR THISSS NONSSSENSSSE. BRETHREN, YOU MAY FEASSST ON THISSS HUMAN PARASSSITE!
HEY, DON'T ALL STAMPEDE AT ONCE - - THERE'S PLENTY OF ME TO GO...AROUND?
ACTUALLY, SCRATCH THAT LAST COMMENT. PLEASE.

GRAAWWR
WHOA! DOWN, BOY -- DOWN!!
OKAY, I NEED TO GET THE GANG-THAT-TIME-FORGOT AWAY FROM THE CAMP AND THE AIRCRAFT. SOOO...
THIS WAY, REPPOS -- FRESH MEAT, ON THE BONE!
AFTER HIM! DON'T LET HIM ESSSCAPE!!
SOME DAY, HUH? LIKE, THE LIZARD'S SICCED REPTILES ON ME BEFORE, LIKE SNAKES AND 'GATORS...
...BUT THESE CRITTERS WOULD GIVE THE HULK A RUN FOR HIS MONEY. NOT THAT HE'S GOT ANY, NATCH--
YIKES!!!
HEY, NO FAIR! LIKE, THIS IS HARD ENOUGH WITHOUT YOU FELLAS TAG-TEAMING!
THOSE RAPTORS ARE FAST. BUT IF I CAN MAKE IT TO THAT HIGH GROUND OVER THERE...

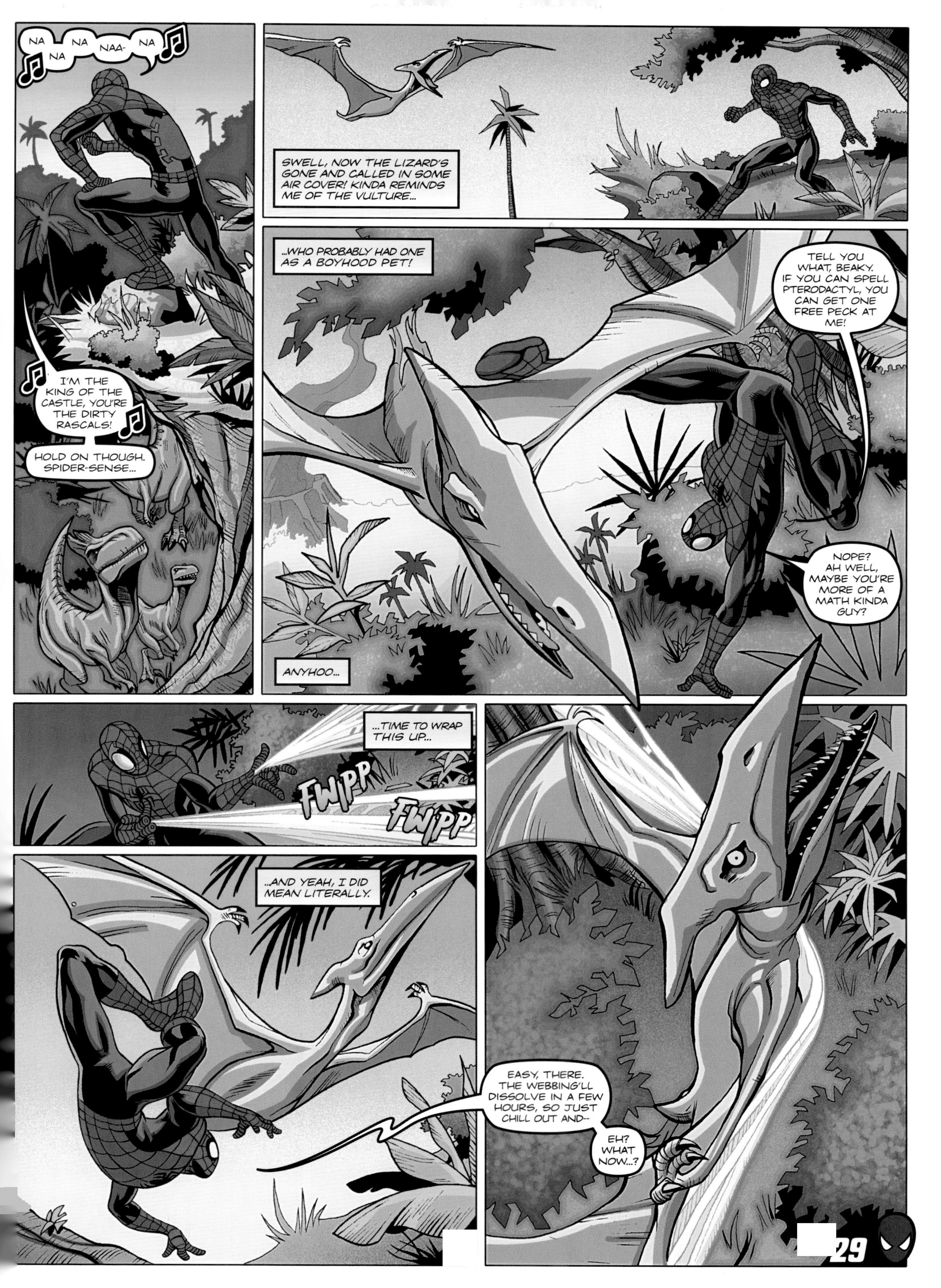
NA NA NA NAA- NA
SWELL, NOW THE LIZARD'S GONE AND CALLED IN SOME AIR COVER! KINDA REMINDS ME OF THE VULTURE...
I'M THE KING OF THE CASTLE, YOU'RE THE DIRTY RASCALS!
HOLD ON THOUGH. SPIDER-SENSE...
...WHO PROBABLY HAD ONE AS A BOYHOOD PET!
TELL YOU WHAT, BEAKY. IF YOU CAN SPELL PTERODACTYL, YOU CAN GET ONE FREE PECK AT ME!
NOPE? AH WELL, MAYBE YOU'RE MORE OF A MATH KINDA GUY?
ANYHOO...
...TIME TO WRAP THIS UP...
FWIPP
FWIPP
...AND YEAH, I DID MEAN LITERALLY.
EASY, THERE. THE WEBBING'LL DISSOLVE IN A FEW HOURS, SO JUST CHILL OUT AND--
EH? WHAT NOW...?

UFF!
THWAAK
YOU SHOULD HAVE STAYED IN THE SSCITY, SSSPIDER-MAN. BECAUSSSE THESSSE JUNGLESSS ARE MY DOMAIN!!
KRUNCH
UNFF!
SSSTILL TWITCHING? WELL, NOT FOR MUCH LONGER!
NGH!
KRASH
NGH!

CONTINUED ON PAGE 34!

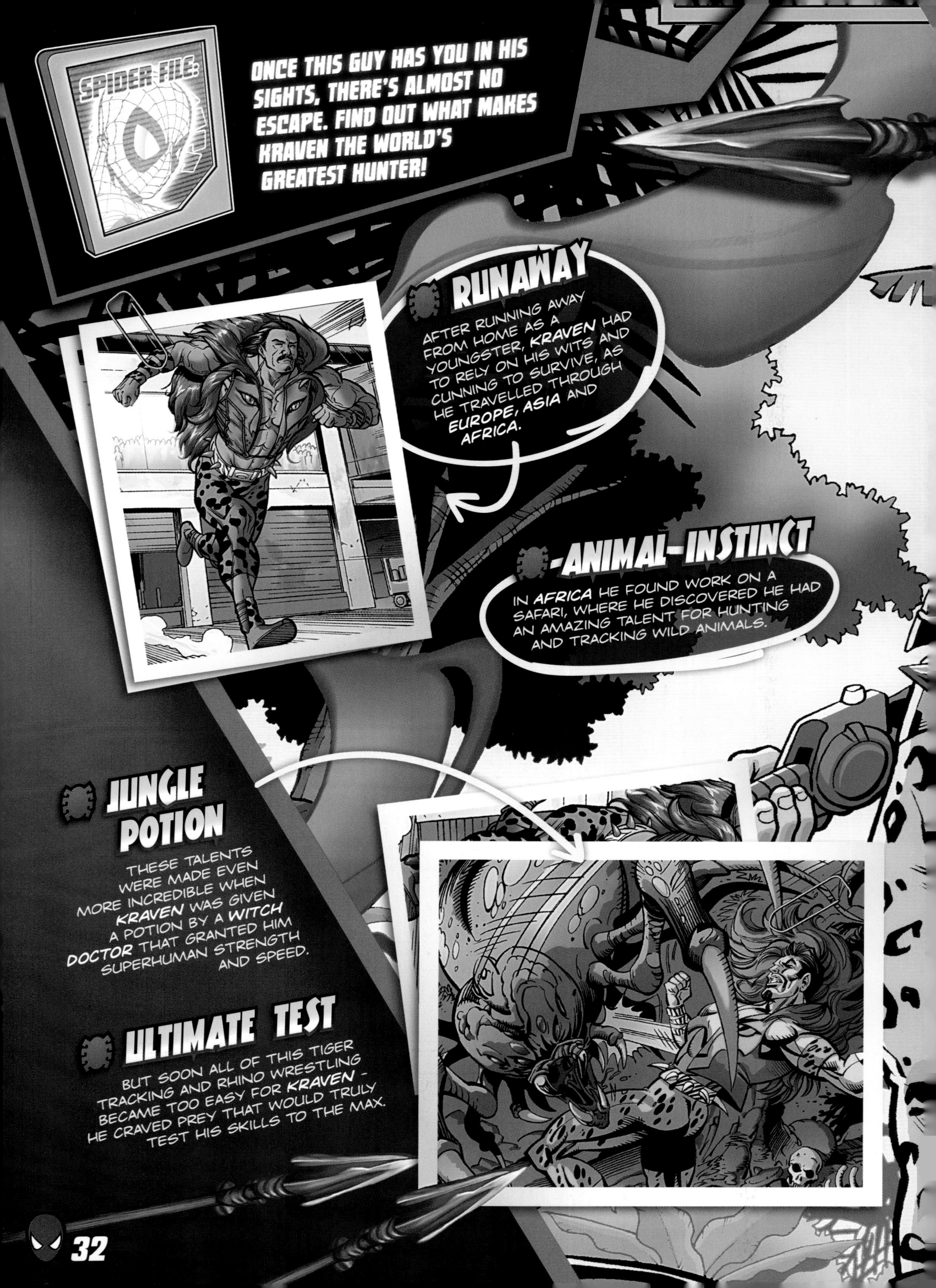

SPIDER-FILE:

ONCE THIS GUY HAS YOU IN HIS SIGHTS, THERE'S ALMOST NO ESCAPE. FIND OUT WHAT MAKES KRAVEN THE WORLD'S GREATEST HUNTER!

RUNAWAY

AFTER RUNNING AWAY FROM HOME AS A YOUNGSTER, ***KRAVEN*** HAD TO RELY ON HIS WITS AND CUNNING TO SURVIVE, AS HE TRAVELLED THROUGH ***EUROPE, ASIA*** AND ***AFRICA.***

ANIMAL INSTINCT

IN ***AFRICA*** HE FOUND WORK ON A SAFARI, WHERE HE DISCOVERED HE HAD AN AMAZING TALENT FOR HUNTING AND TRACKING WILD ANIMALS.

JUNGLE POTION

THESE TALENTS WERE MADE EVEN MORE INCREDIBLE WHEN ***KRAVEN*** WAS GIVEN A POTION BY A ***WITCH DOCTOR*** THAT GRANTED HIM SUPERHUMAN STRENGTH AND SPEED.

ULTIMATE TEST

BUT SOON ALL OF THIS TIGER TRACKING AND RHINO WRESTLING BECAME TOO EASY FOR ***KRAVEN*** - HE CRAVED PREY THAT WOULD TRULY TEST HIS SKILLS TO THE MAX.

KRAVEN THE HUNTER

SPIDER-PREY

AFTER HE ENCOUNTERED **SPIDER-MAN** FOR THE FIRST TIME, **KRAVEN** KNEW HE'D FOUND HIS PREY. FROM THAT MOMENT ON, HE SWORE NOT TO REST UNTIL HE HAD CAPTURED **SPIDEY** AND COMPLETED HIS ULTIMATE HUNT.

ULTIMATE HUNTER!

- Can lift almost 2 tons
- Expert with spears, darts, axes, nets and whips
- Has quicker reflexes than a darting snake
- Can stop a charging bear with one punch
- Can paralyse someone's arm or leg with one devastating nerve punch
- Can run faster than a cheetah

YEP, THE OLD PARKER LUCK'S RUNNING TRUE TO FORM, AND BIG STYLE. 'COS FIRST I GET A PASTING FROM THE LIZARD...
...AND THEN I RUN SMACK DAB INTO KRAVEN HERE - - WHO'D LIKE NOTHING BETTER THAN A SPIDEY-HEAD TROPHY SITTING OVER HIS MANTLEPIECE!
DAY OF THE HUNTER
PENCILS: JOHN ROYLE
INKS: LEE TOWNSEND
COLOURS: JAMES OFFREDI
SCRIPT: FERG HANDLEY
LETTERS: WILL LUCAS
EDITOR: FERG HANDLEY
AH WELL, HERE WE GO THEN...
NARGH!
TZZKK
HOW PREDICTABLE. NOT TO MENTION FUTILE, SPIDER.
THAT'S BETTER. BUT TRY IT AGAIN AND YOU'LL RECEIVE THE MAXIMUM DOSE.

NOW, TELL ME -- WHAT BRINGS YOU HERE TO THE SAVAGE LAND?
CAREFUL, PARKER, DON'T SAY ANYTHING THAT'LL RISK YOUR SECRET IDENTITY...
OKAY, I'LL COME CLEAN... I WAS TRAILING YOU, KRAVINOFF.
NO, THERE'S MORE TO IT THAN THAT. WHO SENT YOU?
COME ON, THINK... FIND SOMETHING BELIEVABLE...
ALRIGHT, ALRIGHT... IT WAS S.H.I.E.L.D.
BLAST, MY DEALINGS WITH THE HELIX CORPORATION WERE SUPPOSED TO BE TOP SECRET!
WHOA, SOUNDS LIKE I STRUCK LUCKY. AND SEEING AS HELIX ARE ONE OF THE SHADIER PLAYERS IN THE BIO-TECH FIELD...
MIND YOU, EVEN NICK FURY DIDN'T HAVE ALL THE DETAILS. BUT HE FIGURED YOU WERE AFTER DINOSAURS... RIGHT?
NO, JUST THEIR DNA. MY EMPLOYERS REQUIRED SAMPLES FOR THEIR RESEARCH PROGRAMME--
--AND WHO BETTER TO OBTAIN THEM THAN THE WORLD'S GREATEST HUNTER?
HOWEVER, I SAW NO POINT IN KILLING SUCH MAGNIFICENT BEASTS. ESPECIALLY WHEN NON-LETHAL METHODS WOULD SUFFICE.
GEE, YOU'RE ALL HEART. STILL, THAT EXPLAINS THE MEGA-TASER, I GUESS.
CORRECT, ALONG WITH ALL THE OTHER HARDWARE THEY SUPPLIED, SUCH AS SCANNERS, MOTION SENSORS AND A HIGH-VELOCITY TRANQUILISER GUN.
AFTER A MONTH'S HUNTING, I HAD ALMOST REACHED MY QUOTA. THEN TODAY, I SAW YOU DEFEATED BY THAT LIZARD CREATURE...

...SO I BROUGHT YOU HERE. NATURALLY, I CONSIDERED UNMASKING YOU, BUT I ONCE VOWED ONLY TO DO SO AFTER I'D BESTED YOU IN COMBAT.
YEAH...
...WELL GOOD LUCK WITH THAT, KRAVINOFF!
UNFF!
FWAK
NO WAY I'M LEAVING WITHOUT DESTROYING THOSE SAMPLES OF HIS.
THE TASER GETS THE SAME TREATMENT, DITTO HIS TRACKING TECH. BUT WHEN I GO TO WEB HIM UP...
DARN, THAT LAST SHOCK MUST'VE JAMMED MY WEB-SHOOTERS UP. THAT'S GONNA BE A DRAWBACK WHEN I FACE THE LIZARD AGAIN.
SPEAKING OF WHICH, I NEED TO GET MOVING. THOSE SCIENTISTS ARE IN SERIOUS DANGER...
...AND JUDGING BY THAT LANDMARK MOUNTAIN, I'M A GOOD TEN MILES AWAY FROM BASE CAMP.
NGH!
THE SPIDER, HE'S GONE...

BUT HE CAN'T ELUDE ME, NOT IN THIS TERRAIN. AND I STILL HAVE ONE VIAL OF JUNGLE POTION REMAINING...
...WHICH WILL ENSURE I HAVE THE NECESSARY STRENGTH TO OVERWHELM HIM!
MAN, I HATE IT HERE. TRAILS KEEP PETERING OUT, AND THERE'S ALL SORTS OF NASTIES LURKING IN THE SHRUBBERY.
UH-OH, SPIDER-SENSE KICKING IN. BUT WHY, I CAN'T SEE ANYTHING--
OY!
THWAAK
YOU AGAIN. THAT DOES IT, MISTER -- FROM NOW ON, I'M CALLING YOU KRAVEN THE STALKER.
UNLIKELY, AS YOU'LL SOON BE--
UNFF!
KRUNCH

NO, THAT WAS MY COMMS DEVICE! I NEEDED IT TO ARRANGE MY EXTRACTION, YOU CRETIN!
SORREE - - NOT!
WHY YOU GIBBERING IMBECILE!
WHOA!!
UFF!
ARGH!
MANAGED TO ROLL WITH IT...
...BUT YEEUCH, THERE'S ONE NASTY SMELL IN THIS GULLY, LIKE ROTTEN OFFAL. AND COME TO THINK OF IT...
...WHAT'S WITH ALL THE COBWEBS?
YOU HAVE TRIED MY PATIENCE ENOUGH, SPIDER. THIS ENDS, NOW!
WOW, NEVER HEARD THAT ONE. WELL, WHAT'RE YOU...
NO, IT CAN'T BE...!!!
...WAITING FOR?

CONTINUED ON PAGE 41

SPIDEY CENTRAL!
More puzzles to set your spider-sense tingling!
DINO DNA!
DIPLODOCUS ✓
IGUANODON
TITANOSAURUS
MEGARAPTOR
BRACHIOSAURUS
DILOPHOSAURUS
TRICERATOPS
GIGANOTOSAURUS
TYRANNOSAURUS
STEGOSAURUS
VELOCIRAPTOR
SPIDEY'S FOUND A PIECE OF PAPER WITH THE DINOSAUR SPECIES KRAVEN WAS COLLECTING DNA FROM, BUT IT'S BEEN TORN UP.
DIPLOD
TRICE
VELO
OCUS
RATOPS
OCIRAPTOR
TYRANN
STEGO
DILOPH
IGUANO
OSAURUS
SAURUS
OSAURUS
DON
PIECE IT TOGETHER, AND PUT A TICK IN THE BOXES NEXT TO THE DINOSAUR NAMES THAT ARE WRITTEN ON IT!
DEADLY SPEARS!
KRAVEN'S THROWN SOME SPEARS AT SPIDEY, BUT ONLY ONE OF THEM IS POISONOUS.
CAN YOU USE THE EXAMPLE TO SPOT WHICH SPEAR HE'S THROWN IS THE POISONOUS ONE?
ANSWER
A
B
C
D
E
F
POISONOUS SPEAR

CONTINUED FROM PAGE 39
THIS IS BAD. BUT WHY HASN'T IT ATTACKED ME YET? UNLESS...
WAIT, THAT'S IT. I'VE GOT SPIDER GENES, SO THERE MUST BE SOME SORT OF PRIMEVAL BOND, LIKE THE LIZARD HAS WITH REPTILES!
KRAVEN THOUGH, HE'S DEFINITELY NOT IN THE CLUB...
SKRR
NARGH!
N-NO! SPIDER-MAN, PLEASE -- DO SOMETHING!!!
IT'S TOO BIG TO FIGHT. BESIDES, I CAN'T RISK IT TURNING ON ME. THAT LEAVES JUST ONE OPTION...
SKRR
...A HUMAN SHIELD!
PHEW, IT'S HESITATING. BUT IT COULD STILL SPRING AT ANY SECOND...
WHAT'RE YOU WAITING FOR, KRAVEN? MOVE, GET THE HECK OUT OF HERE!

YOU HAVE SAVED MY LIFE, SPIDER-MAN. AND KRAVEN NEVER FORGETS A DEBT OF HONOUR.
QUIT YAKKING, WILL YA? IF THE SOUND OF YOUR VOICE BUGS ME, JUST THINK WHAT IT'S DOING TO GOLIATH HERE!
OKAY, THAT'S HIM OUT OF THE WAY. AND I'VE JUST HAD AN IDEA, OF THE SO-CRAZY-IT-MIGHT-JUST-WORK VARIETY...
LISTEN, I KNOW YOU CAN UNDERSTAND ME... SO PLEASE, LET US OUT OF HERE!
SSSILENCE, HUMAN. NOW, YOU ARE THE BAIT...
...FOR IF SSSPIDER-MAN IS SSSTILL ALIVE, NO DOUBT HE WILL TRY TO SSSAVE YOU SSSIMPERING MAMMALS.
AND ONCE HE HASSS MET HISSS END, MY BRETHREN WILL HELP ME RULE THISSS LAND!!
WAIT! SSSOMETHING ISSS HAPPENING...

THAT'S RIGHT, LIZAROONEY -- ANYTHING YOU CAN DO, I CAN DO BETTER!
WOO-HAH!
KATHAAAAAM
WELL, TO BE FAIR, I'VE NOT GOT A TELEPATHIC HOLD ON THIS BABY. BUT AT LEAST IT LET ME MOUNT UP AND MAKE WITH THE REINS.
TO ME, MY BRETHREN! DESSSTROY THISSS ARACHNID ABOMINATION!
LOOKS LIKE HE'S CALLING IN THE GANG. GOT IT COVERED THOUGH...
...THANKS TO KRAVEN DROPPING HIS TRANK GUN BACK AT THE GULLY.
HSSSSS!!!
YEP, I FIGURED THAT IF THE DARTS CAN PENETRATE DINO HIDE, THEY'D DO THE SAME TO THE LIZARD'S.
NOoooooo!!!
SO ALL I HAD TO DO WAS SWAP THE TRANQUILISER PAYLOAD FOR ANTI-SERUM...
NGH!
...AND BOB'S YOUR UNCLE.

PROBLEM IS, MY RIDE'S DECIDED TO MIX IT UP WITH THE CRETACEOUS CREW. NO WAY I'M GETTING IN THE MIDDLE OF THAT RUMBLE...
LATERS, PARTNER. AND YOU PLAY NICE NOW, OKAY.
SKRAAAWR
RIGHT, TIME WE WEREN'T HERE. SO I GRAB CONNORS...
... AND MAKE A BEE-LINE BACK TO MY TENT. OR WHAT'S LEFT OF IT, THAT IS. STILL, MY CLOTHES ARE STILL THERE...
...THEN IT'S STRAIGHT OVER TO THE OTHERS.
PETER, THANK HEAVENS! BUT HOW...
NO TIME FOR THAT, PROFESSOR. WE NEED TO GET TO THE AIRCRAFT, WHILE IT'S STILL IN ONE PIECE.
WELL, WE MAKE IT ABOARD...

...AND THAT'S THAT, WE'RE OUTTA HERE.
THE DOC COMES ROUND A FEW MINUTES LATER, AND WHEN HE HEARS ABOUT THE LIZARD...
THAT'S STRANGE, HIM TURNING UP HERE. BUT ALL I REMEMBER IS TRIPPING OVER A ROOT IN THE JUNGLE, CRACKING MY HEAD AND PASSING OUT.
NOT A BAD COVER STORY. BUT WHAT'S DONE IS DONE, SO...
YEAH, I FOUND YOU UNCONSCIOUS, DOC. BUT WHEN I SAW THE LIZARD AND ALL THOSE DINOS, I WAS TOO SCARED TO DO ANYTHING...
AND STAYED IN HIDING, RIGHT? SENSIBLE MOVE, PARKER... AND IT'S LUCKY FOR US ALL THAT SPIDER-MAN WAS IN THE AREA.
SURE WAS, PROFESSOR. IN FACT, HE GOT ME MOVING AFTER THAT GIANT SPIDER WENT LOCO... THEN HEADED OFF TO DEAL WITH SOME 'KRAVEN' GUY.
PHEW, THAT SHOULD JUST ABOUT COVER IT. AND SPEAKING OF KRAVINOFF, HE MIGHT BE STRANDED DOWN THERE...
...BUT IF THERE'S ONE GUY WHO CAN SURVIVE THE SAVAGE LAND, IT'S HIM!
THE END.

EYE SPIDEY!
PETER
CAN YOU SPOT 10 DIFFERENCES BETWEEN THESE TWO PICTURES ?
AT LAST, SPIDER-LOSER, I HAVE YOU EXACTLY WHERE I WANT YOU!
AW SHUCKS, AND HERE'S ME WITHOUT MY BUCKET AND SPADE!

STORY: SCOTT GRAY ART: JOHN ROSS COLOUR: JAMES OFFREDI LETTERS: TIM WARRAN-SMITH

EDITOR: ED HAMMOND

Daily Bugle
Spider-Man: The True Cause of Global Warming
OH, COME ON! WHO'D BE DUMB ENOUGH TO BELIEVE --

YOU SUCK, WEBHEAD!
YEAH, LEAVE OUR OZONE LAYER ALONE!
HAPPY HOLIDAYS, KIDS.
HOPE SANTA BRINGS YOU A NEW BRAIN...

WHY BOTHER? SERIOUSLY. WHY BOTHER...?
I GET THIS ALL THE TIME. I'M SICK OF BEING THE HUMAN RACE'S CHEW TOY!

HEY, PLANET EARTH! YOU REALLY DON'T WANT ME AROUND, HUH? FINE BY ME! IF THE WORLD DOESN'T NEED SPIDER-MAN, THEN NEITHER DO I!
IF YOU WANT ME TO TOSS THIS OUTFIT IN A DUMPSTER FOR GOOD, JUST GIVE ME ONE LAST SIGN!

YOWZA!!!
WHH-AA--?!!
ZWAK

WHO THE HECK ARE YOU?
I'M MORPH, MUTANT HERO OF A THOUSAND UNIVERSES AND MAN OF A MILLION FACES!
TA-DAAAA!!!
YOU KINDA LOOK LIKE THE CHAMELEON...
PSHAW! HE'S A RANK AMATEUR COMPARED TO ME, MR WEBS -- CHECK THIS OUT...

BOINK
CURSE YOU, SPIDER-MAN! HOLD THE FRONT PAGE! WAX MY MOUSTACHE!
OKAY, STOP, THAT'S JUST CREEPY.

I'M A MEMBER OF THE EXILES! WE'RE A GROUP OF GOOD GUYS WHO TRAVEL THE MULTIVERSE...
WE BATTLE EVILDOERS ACROSS THE INFINITE NUMBER OF PARALLEL UNIVERSES!
PARALLEL UNIVERSES...?

BOINK
YEAH! Y'KNOW, LIKE IN STAR TREK WHEN EVIL MR SPOCK HAD A GOATEE?
OH, RIGHT.

THE THING IS, WE GOT INTO A BIG SCRAP ON EARTH 86749 AND THE OTHER EXILES GOT CAPTURED. I REALLY NEED YOUR HELP TO SAVE MY BUDDIES...
OKAY, MY SPIDER-SENSE ISN'T BUZZING SO I GUESS YOU'RE FOR REAL.... BUT WHY DO YOU NEED ME?

'CAUSE YOU'RE THE MISSING INGREDIENT, DUDE! C'MON, LET'S HUSTLE!!!
HEY, WAIT A MIN—
ZWAKK

-UTE...?
HUH? WE DIDN'T GO ANYWHERE!
AU CONTRAIRE, MONSIEUR ARACHNID... OBSERVE...

THAT'S WHERE THE EXILES ARE BEING HELD CAPTIVE...
THE GOBLIN CITADEL!
OOOHHH, NO -- LET ME GUESS: IT'S OWNED BY A GUY WITH A THING FOR GREEN AND PURPLE, AND HAIR LIKE A RUSTY BRILLO PAD, RIGHT...?
YUP!

NAAARGH!
THAT CAME FROM BELOW!

SSSSSTOP IN THE NAME OF THE GREEN GOBLIN!
YOUR DEFIANCE ENDSSSS TONIGHT, HUMAN SSSCUM!

HEY, WHAT HAPPENED TO "PROTECT AND SERVE", BOYS?
STOP! HAMMER TIME!
THWOK
FWAAK
UNFF!

THESE COPS LOOK JUST LIKE THE LIZARD! THEY'RE NOT AS STRONG, BUT THEY'VE BEEN CHANGED BY THE SAME SERUM!
THIS SHOULD HOLD 'EM FOR A WHILE...
FWIP

YOU OKAY, BUDDY?
I'LL LIVE. THANK YOU, M'BOY. IT'S GOOD TO KNOW THERE ARE STILL MEN OUT THERE FIGHTING. WE'RE NOT LICKED YET...

THE NAME'S J JONAH JAMESON.
WHO ARE YOU?
I... UM...
OBOY.

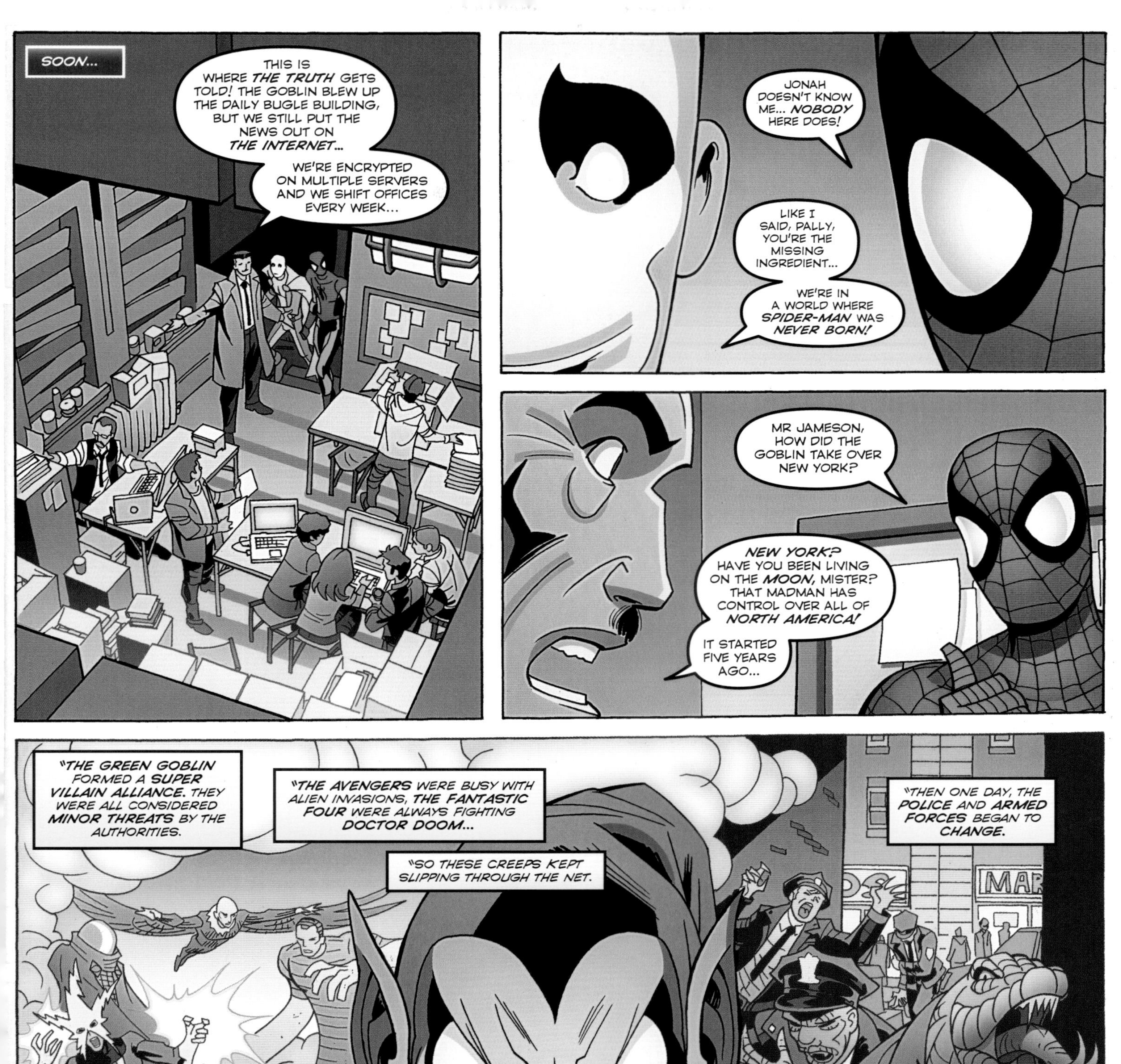

SOON...
THIS IS WHERE THE TRUTH GETS TOLD! THE GOBLIN BLEW UP THE DAILY BUGLE BUILDING, BUT WE STILL PUT THE NEWS OUT ON THE INTERNET...
WE'RE ENCRYPTED ON MULTIPLE SERVERS AND WE SHIFT OFFICES EVERY WEEK...
JONAH DOESN'T KNOW ME... NOBODY HERE DOES!
LIKE I SAID, PALLY, YOU'RE THE MISSING INGREDIENT...
WE'RE IN A WORLD WHERE SPIDER-MAN WAS NEVER BORN!
MR JAMESON, HOW DID THE GOBLIN TAKE OVER NEW YORK?
NEW YORK? HAVE YOU BEEN LIVING ON THE MOON, MISTER? THAT MADMAN HAS CONTROL OVER ALL OF NORTH AMERICA!
IT STARTED FIVE YEARS AGO...

"THE GREEN GOBLIN FORMED A SUPER VILLAIN ALLIANCE. THEY WERE ALL CONSIDERED MINOR THREATS BY THE AUTHORITIES.
"THE AVENGERS WERE BUSY WITH ALIEN INVASIONS, THE FANTASTIC FOUR WERE ALWAYS FIGHTING DOCTOR DOOM...
"SO THESE CREEPS KEPT SLIPPING THROUGH THE NET.
"THEN ONE DAY, THE POLICE AND ARMED FORCES BEGAN TO CHANGE.
"A BIO-FORMULA HAD BEEN PLACED IN THEIR WATER SUPPLIES. AMERICA WAS LEFT DEFENCELESS OVERNIGHT.
"THE GOBLIN HAD AN INSTANT ARMY.

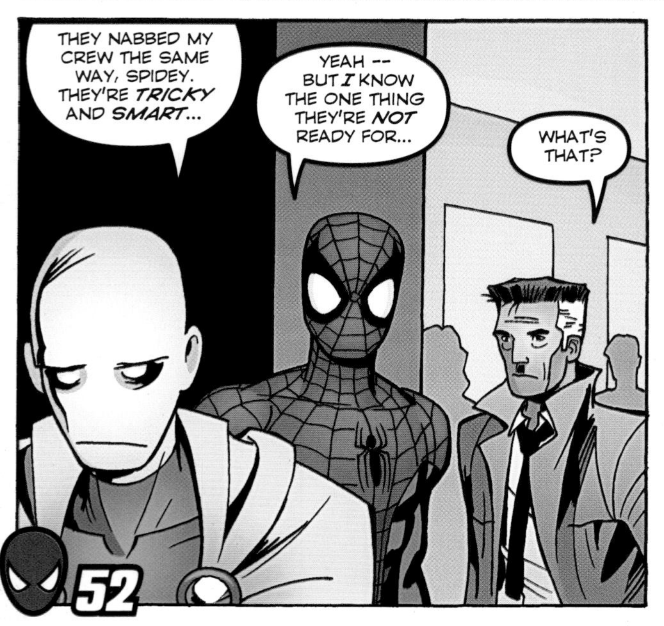

CONTINUED ON PAGE 54...

TOWER OF TERROR!
Isn't it always the way, folks?! You wait hours for one Super Villain and then thirteen turn up at once! See if you can help Spidey defeat them all by spotting where in the skyscraper their names are hidden? Good luck!
A M H S I O S P A
G E N H E Q Z I W
C Q A O Z M X G S
W E D C C O V R F
R T G K B R N E H
Y M U E J B M E K
S C O R P I O N I
O L P N Q U A G S
Z X S W E S E O U
D M C V F V N B P
R T Y G B I N L O
N H Y S H U J I T
O M K R T I O N C
E L P Q A E Z X O
L S W E D C R V R
E R U T L U V I D
M N A M D N A S O
A R T G B N H Y U
H O B G O B L I N
C J M D R A Z I L
SHOCKER
LIZARD
CHAMELEON
MORBIUS
MYSTERIO
VULTURE
SANDMAN
HOBGOBLIN
VENOM
DR. OCTOPUS
SCORPION
RHINO
GREEN GOBLIN
53

...CONTINUED FROM PAGE 52

AT LAST... A SUPER-POWERED ARMY AT MY COMMAND! HOW LONG WILL DOCTOR DOOM WITHSTAND SUCH A FORCE?
HOW LONG BEFORE THE RED SKULL AND THE MANDARIN FALL TO MY POWER?
HOW LONG BEFORE THE GREEN GOBLIN REIGNS SUPREME OVER THE ENTIRE WORLD?!

IS THAT A TRICK QUESTION, YOUR CRAZINESS? 'CAUSE MY GUESS IS HALF-PAST NEVER!
KRAAAAASH
WHAT--?!

WHO ISSSS THISSS FOOL?
NO IDEA! HE'S MOVIN' LIKE SOME KINDA... MAN-SPIDER!

I'M THE GUY WHO KNOWS ALL YOUR POWERS, ALL YOUR TACTICS, ALL YOUR TRICKS...
BUT YOU DON'T KNOW ME AT ALL, DO YOU?
THWAAAK
UNFF!
OKAY, QUICK PRIMER: I HAVE THE PROPORTIONATE STRENGTH AND SPEED OF A SPIDER...
SSSSS!
CHOKK

I'VE GOT A SPIDER-SENSE THAT WARNS ME AGAINST ILLUSIONS TOO! NEAT, HUH?
KRRRK
UFF!

YOU'RE GONNA FRY, YOU FREAK!
HERE'S A FUN FACT, ELECTRO -- I KNOW YOU SHOOT ELECTRICAL CHARGES OF UP TO 100,000 VOLTS...

...THEY REACH AROUND 30,000 DEGREES CENTIGRADE...
ARGH!
KAZZZT

...AND THAT'S HOT ENOUGH TO FUSE SAND INTO GLASS!

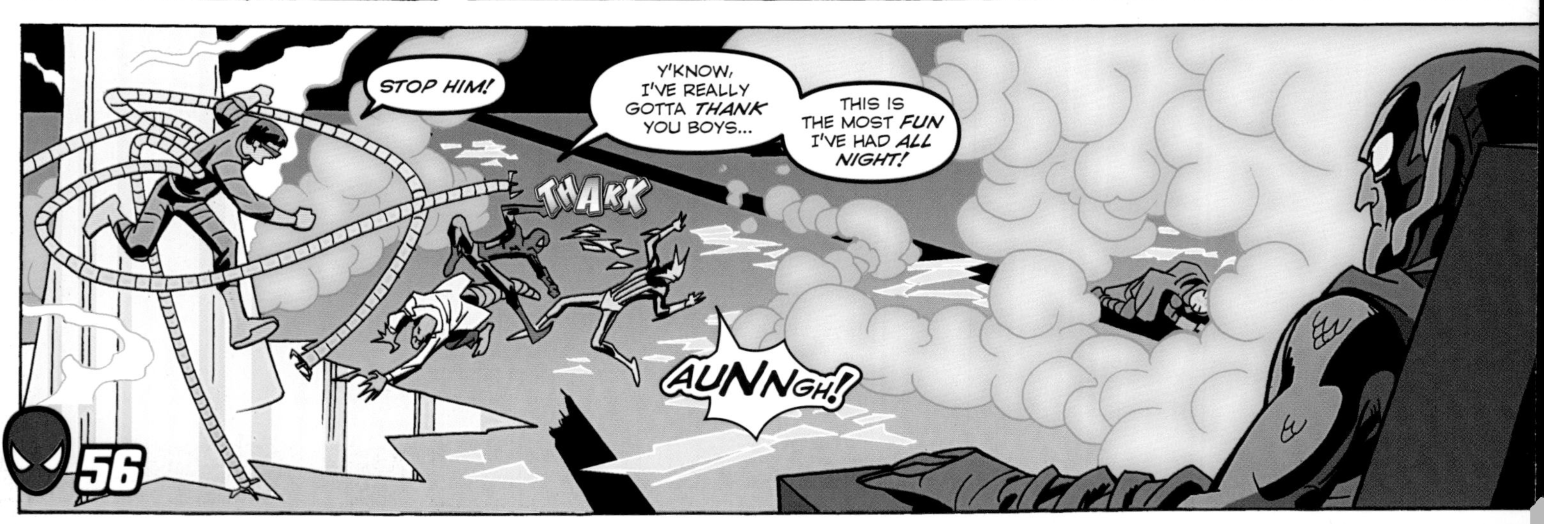
STOP HIM!
Y'KNOW, I'VE REALLY GOTTA THANK YOU BOYS...
THIS IS THE MOST FUN I'VE HAD ALL NIGHT!
THAKK
AUNNGH!

TINKERER, WE'RE UNDER ATTACK! SOME GUY'S BROKEN THROUGH THE CITADEL'S DEFENCES! HE'S UP IN THE THRONE ROOM AND HE'S BEATING EVERYONE!
CHAMELEON? I THOUGHT YOU WERE IN ALABAMA...

BOINK
FWAAK
HEY, YOU'RE RIGHT!
HE IS!

UGGH! WHAT IS THIS GUNK?!
WHAT, DID I FORGET TO MENTION THE WEBBING? SORRY, VULTURE! IT'S A LONG-CHAIN POLYMER FIBRE THAT EXPANDS --
OH, NEVER MIND...
FWIP

...I'LL LET DOC OCK EXPLAIN IT TO YOU!
OOOF!!!
FLUUUMP

YOU IMBECILES, HE'S MAKING FOOLS OF YOU ALL!
GUARDS!!!

CRUSH THIS INSECT!
SSSSSSSSSSSSSSSSSSSSS
SSSSSSSSSSS!!!

I DON'T CARE HOW FAST YOU ARE, YOU CAN'T OUTFIGHT US ALL!
I WASN'T PLANNING TO. Y'SEE, I WAS JUST THE WARM-UP ACT FOR YOU BOZOS...

...HERE COMES THE MAIN ATTRACTION!
ZAAAAKK
ARGH!

AVENGERS ASSEMBLE!
IT'S CLOBBERIN' TIME!
EXILES... UH... EXCITE!

YOU'RE GONNA NEED A DYNAMITE LAWYER, LIZARD!
HERE'S ONE I OWE YOU, ELECTRO!
THRAMM
ZWAK
UNFF!

THESE ARE MY EXILES BUDDIES, DUDE! BLINK, POLARIS AND BEAST!
BIG FAN, SPIDEY!
THANKS FOR THE HELP!
FWOKK
YOUR ASSISTANCE WAS INVALUABLE!
ZZHHAK

KRRAK
BIRD SEASON JUST OPENED, VULCHY!
HEY, NEW GUY! WE GOT YOU TO THANK FOR SPRINGIN' US?
SHUDK
NOW THAT YOU MENTION IT, YEAH! NICE TO MEET YOU ALL...
I'M YOUR FRIENDLY NEIGHBOURHOOD SPIDER-MAN!

NOOOO!!!
YOU'VE DESTROYED EVERYTHING! MY EMPIRE -- MY DREAMS!
ALL YOU EVER MADE WERE NIGHTMARES, GOBLIN!
ZAAAK

YOU'VE BROUGHT NOTHING BUT FEAR TO THIS WORLD...
BUT I KNOW YOU, AND I KNOW WHAT YOU'RE SCARED OF!
THWAK

FACE THE TRUTH -- THE GREEN GOBLIN IS A LIE...

...YOU'RE NORMAN OSBORN!
ARGH!

IT'S OVER.
OSBORN...
OSBORN...
OSBORN...

DAWN...
I GAVE MR FANTASTIC THE FORMULA TO REVERSE THE LIZARD SERUM -- YOU SHOULD HAVE YOUR POLICE FORCE BACK PRETTY SOON...
YOU ACCOMPLISHED MORE IN ONE NIGHT THAN THE REST OF US DID IN FIVE YEARS. AMAZING!

I'VE NEVER APPROVED OF COSTUMED VIGILANTES -- BUT YOU'VE CHANGED MY MIND, SON.
I WAS WONDERING...
WOULD YOU TELL ME WHO YOU REALLY ARE?

WOW. JUST WHEN I THOUGHT THIS TRIP COULDN'T GET ANY CRAZIER...
BUT THIS ISN'T "MY" JONAH. WHY NOT?
WELL... UM...
OKAY.

MY NAME IS PETER PARKER.
I ONCE MADE A REALLY BIG MISTAKE, AND I LOST SOMEONE DEAR TO ME. I'VE BEEN TRYING TO BE WORTHY OF HIS MEMORY EVER SINCE.

WELL, I THINK HE'D BE MIGHTY PROUD OF YOU TODAY, PETER. IT'S AN HONOUR TO KNOW YOU.
KEEP FIGHTING THE GOOD FIGHT.

READY TO HEAD BACK TO YOUR EARTH, SPIDEY?
YEAH, SURE, MORPH... JUST LET ME PUT MY BRAINS BACK INTO MY HEAD...

SO HERE I AM, BACK HOME. AND OKAY, NOTHING'S REALLY CHANGED -- I'M STILL JOE PUBLIC'S FAVOURITE WHIPPING BOY...
BUT LOOK WHAT HAPPENED WHEN I WASN'T AROUND.
I GUESS THE WORLD REALLY DOES NEED A SPIDER-MAN!
Daily Bugle
Spider-Man: The True Cause of Global Warming
THE END.

ANSWERS

12 SHAPE SHIFTING!

C A B

NAME & SHAME! FLINT MARKO

24 SPIDEY CENTRAL!

CODE 83904

DOYOUTHINK-HESAURUS?

NUMBER OF DINOSAURS 10

40 SPIDEY CENTRAL!

DINO DNA!

DIPLODOCUS, IGUANADON, DILOPHOSAURUS, TRICERATOPS, STEGOSAURUS, VELOCIRAPTOR, TYRANNOSAURUS

DEADLY SPEARS!

ANSWER E

46 EYE SPIDEY

53 TOWER OF TERROR!